For When I'm Gone

End-of-Life Planner Journal to Organize Your Belongings, Business Affairs, and Last Wishes

Jeffrey Mason

Hear Your Story Books

HEAR YOUR
STORY

ISBN: 978-1-955034-39-5

Contents

USING THIS BOOK **6**

A CHECKLIST OF WHAT TO PREPARE **9**

Health Care Power of Attorney/Health Care Agent 9
Living Will 10
Do Not Resuscitate (DNR) Orders 11
A Last Will and Testament 12
Funeral Pre-planning and Prepayment 12
Organize Your Documents 14

MY PERSONAL INFORMATION **18**

MY MEDICAL INFORMATION **27**

Physician and Dentist Contact Information 28
Medical History 37
My Allergies and Reactions 38

MY COMPUTER AND INTERNET ACCOUNTS **41**

Password Manager 41
My password manager login information: 42
Smartphone login: 43
My computer login information 43
Primary email addresses and accounts 43
Social media accounts with login information 44
Important websites with login information: 48

BUSINESS & FINANCIAL **55**

My bank account information: 59
My credit card information: 61
My investment accounts: 64

Safe deposit box: 68
Debts or judgements owed to me: 69
My Dependents: 73
My Pets: 78

MY INSTRUCTIONS FOR WHEN I PASS 81

Planning Your Celebration of You 82
In case of my death, these are my wishes: 85
I would like these individuals notified: 93
Writing Your Own Eulogy 106

ABOUT ME 114

About Me: My Birth and Me as a Baby 117
About Me: A Few Things 121
About Me: Memories of My Childhood 125
About Me: My High School Years 133
About Me: Next Steps 143
About Me: My Parents 149
About Me: My Grandparents 163
About Me: My Siblings 169
About Me: My Marriage/My Partner 175
About Me: My Children 179
About Me: My Grandchildren 185
About Me: My Life Experiences 189

I AM GRATEFUL FOR... 199

LETTERS 203

GLOSSARY 214

Using This Book

"Death never takes a wise man by surprise;
he is always ready to go." – Jean de la Fontaine

The inevitable of life is that life will end.

While the bluntness of this statement may cause gloom and unease, it's intended to encourage action.

My father had a talent for life and living. He was always in motion, learning, creating, and building. Each day was an opportunity, and he wasted none of it.

It seemed impossible when he passed, and denial took the place of grief.

Reality eventually arrived with the realization that there was no preparation for life without him, and we needed a plan to manage his and Mom's affairs. We spent days digging through boxes and drawers to find needed documents and hours upon hours on hold and being endlessly transferred to gain access to accounts.

Things eventually got back on schedule despite a few late bills.

This book tells you what your family will need and serves as a secure place to record these things for them. Doing this now will help you continue taking care of the people you love, even after you're gone.

There is also a section to guide you in sharing your wishes for how you want your passing to be acknowledged and your life celebrated. Knowing what you want will help make a difficult time a bit easier for your family.

The last section is where you can share your stories and write your fondest memories. Creating this heirloom of you and your experiences will be a gift to your loved ones and generations to come.

This book and its contents are not intended to provide legal or financial advice or act as or replace the use of a licensed attorney, estate planner, or financial advisor.
We strongly recommend consulting with licensed professionals to manage your legal and financial affairs.

"Cherish
your yesterdays,
dream your tomorrows
and live your todays."
– Author Unknown

A Checklist of What to Prepare

While not applicable to every situation, the below list covers the documents typically needed to manage one's affairs. To ensure the coverage of your situation, we recommend working with an estate attorney and financial planner.

Create and Delegate Your Power of Attorney

A power of attorney is when you legally delegate one or more individuals to act on your behalf. This can include making financial or healthcare decisions if you become incapacitated or have passed.

In most situations, the person/persons appointed are a spouse, family member, or close friend. The critical thing is it is someone you trust. It is also important to assign a backup person in case the first cannot act for whatever reason.

Health Care Power of Attorney/Health Care Agent

A healthcare power of attorney allows you to empower one or more individuals to make medical care decisions for you in the event you cannot. A health care agent or proxy is who you name as your medical decision-maker and who will ensure your wishes be met.

Once you have selected a health care agent, have a medical power of attorney created. If you don't have an attorney, you can use an online service. Options include:

- Legalzoom (www.legalzoom.com)
- Rocket Lawyer (www.rocketlawyer.com)
- Law Depot (www.lawdepot.com/us/estate/living-will-medical-power-of-attorney)

Notify your family and doctors that you have a health care agent and medical power of attorney. Provide your family with a copy and place the original in a safe, accessible place.

Living Will

A living will (also known as an **Advance Directive**) is a legal declaration of your wishes for your medical care if you cannot communicate them yourself.

Having a living will can be an invaluable guide for your doctors while also freeing your loved ones from needing to make tough decisions about your care. Because the rules covering living wills vary from location to location, it is important to get legal guidance when creating one. Options for creating a living will include:

- Legalzoom (www.legalzoom.com/articles/how-to-create-a-living-will-in-3-simple-steps)
- Rocket Lawyer (www.rocketlawyer.com/family-and-personal/health-and-medical/healthcare-decisions/document/living-will)
- Nolo (www.nolo.com/legal-encyclopedia/how-write-living-will.html)

Once created, keep the original copy in a safe location and provide a copy to your health care agent, doctor, and family.

You should revisit your living will at regular intervals or if there is a change in your health care agent, marital status, or overall health.

Do Not Resuscitate (DNR) Orders

A DNR is your notification to your medical care team to not provide life support or resuscitation. This would include the use of cardiac drugs or administration of chest compressions.

A medical power of attorney or living will is not required to have a DNR. You just need to communicate your wishes to your doctor and have it added to your medical record.

A Last Will and Testament

A Last Will and Testament is the primary legal document used to determine the management and distribution of someone's assets upon their passing. It can also address the custody of dependents and special circumstances, such as the care of an aging parent.

Included is the naming of the will's executor, the person who ensures the distribution of assets follows its provisions.

Having a will is critical if you have assets or children. Passing away without a will results in the court system determining the distribution of your assets and the guardianship of any dependents.

While there are several online services that can create a will, it is advisable to work with an attorney. Doing so will help ensure it meets your local legal requirements, helping it survive if challenged.

Funeral Pre-planning and Prepayment

This is working with a funeral home to decide the details of your arrangements. A practical benefit of pre-planning is it helps to understand, plan for, and potentially control costs.

The more emotional benefit is that planning now will relieve your family of the burden of having to plan everything later.

Your plan can simply cover your preferences for burial or cremation and whether you want a funeral or memorial service. It can also cover every element of your ceremony, from the music played to who would offer a eulogy.

One thing to understand is that “pre-planning” does not require “prepaying.”

It is often recommended to avoid paying for services ahead of time, as it is hard to predict future circumstances. Examples of things that could happen include the funeral home going out of business, you moving to another area, or a later change in how you want your passing handled.

One alternate is to set up a “payable-on-death” bank account which would release to your account beneficiary to be used to funeral costs.

Payable-on-death accounts are subject to communality property rules, making it important to work with an estate attorney to ensure it fits your circumstances.

Organize Your Documents

The checklist below includes what you should organize and store in a secure and accessible location. Be sure to include those of your spouse/partner and any dependent(s) (if applicable).

- ☐ Last Will and Testament
- ☐ Living Trust documents
- ☐ Living Will
- ☐ Durable Powers of Attorney documents
- ☐ Health Care Powers of Attorney
- ☐ Birth Certificate
- ☐ Marriage Certificate/Domestic Partner Agreement
- ☐ Divorce papers
- ☐ Social Security Card
- ☐ Passport
- ☐ Titles to property and assets
- ☐ Military Records and Veteran's Affairs file number
- ☐ Retirement plan documents (IRA, 401(k), 403(b), etc.)
- ☐ Deferred compensation and stock option agreements
- ☐ Pension and profit-sharing
- ☐ Mutual fund and brokerage account information

- [ ] Any Business and/or partnership agreements
- [ ] Life insurance policies
- [ ] Medical, homeowners, and auto insurance policies
- [ ] Disability and umbrella policies
- [ ] Long-term care insurance policies
- [ ] Annuity policies
- [ ] Bank account information
- [ ] Tax returns for the last three years
- [ ] Current year tax records
- [ ] Employee benefits program information
- [ ] Loan documents
- [ ] Credit cards information
- [ ] This book (completed)

Be sure to use a licensed attorney and financial advisor for verification that your affairs are in order and all legal documents follow local laws and regulations.

Share and Communicate

Once you have organized your affairs and verified, they are in order, sit down with your family and discuss each item and where it is located.

Discuss who you have asked to serve as your executor and Health Care Agent, and who is on any durable and health care powers of attorney. Cover each person's responsibilities and what you have asked them to do.

Review your wishes for what happens when you pass. This can be very emotional for everyone involved, so be patient and listen.

There is a chance they may have differing opinions than what you have decided. If this occurs, explain your choices, and provide the opportunity for everyone to weigh in.

Keep in mind that what you are doing now means they won't have to do it later.

"There will be
two dates
on your tombstone
and all that's gonna
matter is that
little dash between 'em."
– Kevin Welch

My Personal Information

My full name:

My full name at birth:

Other names I am known by:

My Social Security number:

My driver's license number (include issuing state):

My passport number:

My birth date:

My birthplace:

My legal residence address:

My mailing address:

My P.O. Box number and its location (include where the mailbox key can be found):

My marital status:

My spouse's/partner's name:

Spouse's/partner's birthdate and place of birth:

Date and place of marriage:

I am a veteran (Yes or No):

The branch of the military I served in:

Years served:

Highest rank reached:

Discharge status:

For my home phone...

- Phone number: ______________________________
- Voicemail password: ______________________________

For my mobile phone...

- Phone number: ______________________________
- Lock screen password: ______________________________
- Voicemail password: ______________________________

Other phone number with the voicemail password:

- Phone number: ______________________________
- Voicemail password: ______________________________

Other phone number with the voicemail password:

- Phone number: ______________________________
- Voicemail password: ______________________________

Other phone number with the voicemail password:

- Phone number: ______________________________
- Voicemail password: ______________________________

The location of the following items is...

My birth certificate:

My marriage license:

My social security card:

My passport:

My address book:

Other documents and their location (examples include mortgage documents, divorce papers, etc.):

(continued):

“The saddest
summary of a life
contains three
descriptions:
could have,
might have, and
should have.”
– Louis E. Boone

My Medical Information

My medical insurance policy information:

- Provider: ______________________________
- Policy number: ______________________________
- Website: ______________________________
- Website username: ______________________________
- Website password: ______________________________
- Phone number: ______________________________

Location of my health insurance card:

____

My blood type:

____

Organ donor status (Yes or No) and where it is indicated (driver's license, living will, etc.):

____

____

Physician and Dentist Contact Information

Primary Physician name, address, contact number:

My preferred hospital's name and location:

My preferred pharmacy's name and location:

Specialist name, address, contact number:

Specialist name, address, contact number:

Specialist name, address, contact number:

Specialist name, address, contact number:

Specialist name, address, contact number:

Dentist name, address, contact number:

Additional information on medical providers:

My health care agent is:

____

____

Their contact information is...

Address:

____

____

____

____

Phone numbers where they can be reached:

____

____

The location of the official copy of my medical power of attorney is:

____

____

It was executed on this date:

___

The document was signed by:

___

My medical power of attorney was completed using this attorney/legal service (if the document was created using an online legal service, include the website address and your login and password information):

___

___

___

___

___

Individuals who have a copy of my medical power of attorney include...

- Name: ____________________
- Contact number: ____________________
- Name: ____________________
- Contact number: ____________________

- Name: ____________________
- Contact number: ____________________

- Name: ____________________
- Contact number: ____________________

- Name: ____________________
- Contact number: ____________________

- Name: ____________________
- Contact number: ____________________

The location of the official copy of my living will is:

It was executed on this date and signed by:

The document was completed by this attorney/legal service:

Their contact information is (if the document was created using an online legal service, include the website address and your login and password information):

Individuals who have a copy of my living will include...

- Name: ______________________________
- Contact number: ______________________________

- Name: ______________________________
- Contact number: ______________________________

- Name: ______________________________
- Contact number: ______________________________
- Name: ______________________________
- Contact number: ______________________________

I have a Do Not Resuscitate (DNR) order (Yes or No):

____

I have a Do Not Intubate (DNI) order (Yes or No):

____

These documents can be found in this place:

____

____

Medical History

My medical history includes (check all that apply):

- ☐ Alzheimer's.
- ☐ Dementia.
- ☐ Cancer. Type? ______________________________
- ☐ Clotting disorder. Type? ______________________
- ☐ Diabetes. Type? ____________________________
- ☐ Gastrointestinal condition. Type? ______________
- ☐ Heart disease. Type? ________________________
- ☐ High blood pressure.
- ☐ High cholesterol.
- ☐ Kidney disease. Type? _______________________
- ☐ Lung disease. Type? _________________________
- ☐ Mental health diagnosis. Type? ______________
- ☐ Osteoporosis.
- ☐ Stroke. Number of incidents? _______________

My Allergies and Reactions

My known allergies and the reaction each causes are as follows:

Additional important medical information that should be shared:

"Life is a journey
with problems to solve,
lessons to learn,
but most of all,
experiences to enjoy."
– Author Unknown

My Computer and Internet Accounts

Password Manager

A great way to securely store your website logins and passwords is to use a password manager.

A password manager is a software tool that encrypts and securely stores your login information for the websites you use. Using the highest levels of digital security technology available, they prevent hackers and others from accessing your login credentials while also making it unnecessary for you to remember or write down login information for each account.

Because password managers automatically log you into your accounts when visiting the website, you only have one master password to remember (the one for the password manager).

The added benefit of using a password manager is that it is a simple and effective way to provide your designated person access to all your online accounts after you pass. All they need is to know the password manager you use and have your login information for that one account.

The most popular password managers available include:

- LastPass (lastpass.com)
- Dashlane (dashlane.com)
- LogMeOnce (logmeonce.com)
- 1Password (1password.com)
- Keeper (keepersecurity.com)
- Bitwarden (bitwarden.com)

My password manager login information:

- I am using this password manager:

____

- Website:

____

- Username:

____

- Master password:

____

Smartphone login:

- Smartphone lock screen password: ______________________

My computer login information:

- Computer location: ______________________
- Computer username: ______________________
- Computer password: ______________________

Second computer...

- Computer location: ______________________
- Computer username: ______________________
- Computer password: ______________________

Primary email addresses and accounts

- Email address: ______________________
- Password: ______________________

- Email address: ______________________
- Password: ______________________

Social media accounts with login information

Upon my passing, I would like the following message posted to the social media accounts I have indicated below.

Social media accounts with login information (examples include Pinterest, Instagram, Facebook, Twitter, TikTok, Reddit, etc.):

- Website address: ______________________________
- Username: ______________________________
- Password: ______________________________
- Post my message on this account? Yes ☐ No ☐
- Would you like this account closed? If yes, how long after your passing would you like it left open?

Social media account with login information:

- Website address: ______________________________
- Username: ______________________________
- Password: ______________________________
- Post my message on this account? Yes ☐ No ☐
- Would you like this account closed? If yes, how long after your passing would you like it left open?

____

Social media account with login information:

- Website address: ______________________________
- Username: ______________________________
- Password: ______________________________
- Post my message on this account? Yes ☐ No ☐
- Would you like this account closed? If yes, how long after your passing would you like it left open?

Social media account with login information:

- Website address: ______________________________
- Username: ______________________________
- Password: ______________________________
- Post my message on this account? Yes ☐ No ☐
- Would you like this account closed? If yes, how long after your passing would you like it left open?

____

____

Important websites with login information:

(If not using a password manager)

Website address: ______________________________

- Username: ______________________________
- Password: ______________________________
- Close upon my death? Yes ☐ No ☐

Website address: ______________________________

- Username: ______________________________
- Password: ______________________________
- Close upon my death? Yes ☐ No ☐

Website address: ______________________________

- Username: ______________________________
- Password: ______________________________
- Close upon my death? Yes ☐ No ☐

Website address: ______________________

- Username: ______________________
- Password: ______________________
- Close upon my death? Yes ☐ No ☐

Website address: ______________________

- Username: ______________________
- Password: ______________________
- Close upon my death? Yes ☐ No ☐

Website address: ______________________

- Username: ______________________
- Password: ______________________
- Close upon my death? Yes ☐ No ☐

Website address: ______________________

- Username: ______________________
- Password: ______________________
- Close upon my death? Yes ☐ No ☐

Website address: ______________________

- Username: ______________________
- Password: ______________________
- Close upon my death? Yes☐ No ☐

Website address: ______________________

- Username: ______________________
- Password: ______________________
- Close upon my death? Yes☐ No ☐

Website address: ______________________

- Username: ______________________
- Password: ______________________
- Close upon my death? Yes☐ No ☐

Website address: ______________________

- Username: ______________________
- Password: ______________________
- Close upon my death? Yes☐ No ☐

Website address: ______________________________

- Username: ______________________________
- Password: ______________________________
- Close upon my death? Yes ☐ No ☐

Website address: ______________________________

- Username: ______________________________
- Password: ______________________________
- Close upon my death? Yes ☐ No ☐

Website address: ______________________________

- Username: ______________________________
- Password: ______________________________
- Close upon my death? Yes ☐ No ☐

Website address: ______________________________

- Username: ______________________________
- Password: ______________________________
- Close upon my death? Yes ☐ No ☐

Website address: ______________________________

- Username: ______________________________
- Password: ______________________________
- Close upon my death? Yes ☐ No ☐

Website address: ______________________________

- Username: ______________________________
- Password: ______________________________
- Close upon my death? Yes ☐ No ☐

Website address: ______________________________

- Username: ______________________________
- Password: ______________________________
- Close upon my death? Yes ☐ No ☐

Website address: ______________________________

- Username: ______________________________
- Password: ______________________________
- Close upon my death? Yes ☐ No ☐

Website address: ______________________________

- Username: ______________________________
- Password: ______________________________
- Close upon my death? Yes ☐ No ☐

Website address: ______________________________

- Username: ______________________________
- Password: ______________________________
- Close upon my death? Yes ☐ No ☐

Website address: ______________________________

- Username: ______________________________
- Password: ______________________________
- Close upon my death? Yes ☐ No ☐

Website address: ______________________________

- Username: ______________________________
- Password: ______________________________
- Close upon my death? Yes ☐ No ☐

“The purpose of life
is not to be happy.
It is to be useful,
to be honorable,
to be compassionate,
to have it make
some difference
that you have lived
and lived well.”
– Ralph Waldo Emerson

Business & Financial

The executor of my will's name and contact information:

My appointed financial power of attorney and their contact information is:

The location of the original copy of my will is:

The location of my power of attorney documents is:

My attorney's name and contact information:

My accountant's name and contact information:

My tax information is with (name and how to contact):

Copies of my tax records can also be found here:

My online tax account:

Company/Firm name:

____

____

Account online username: _______________________

Password: ____________________________________

I have a life insurance policy with these companies:

____

____

____

____

My life insurance policies can be found here:

____

____

____

My bank account information:

Bank name:

Account type:

Account number:

Account online username:

Password:

Bank name:

Account type:

Account number:

Account online username:

Password:

My bank account information:

Bank name:

____

____

Account type: ______________________________

Account number: ______________________________

Account online username: ______________________________

Password: ______________________________

Bank name:

____

____

Account type: ______________________________

Account number: ______________________________

Account online username: ______________________________

Password: ______________________________

My credit card information:

Credit card company name:

____

____

Card type (AmEx, Visa, etc.): ____________________

Account number: __________________________

Account online username: ____________________

Password: ______________________________

Credit card company name:

____

____

Card type (AmEx, Visa, etc.): ____________________

Account number: __________________________

Account online username: ____________________

Password: ______________________________

Credit card company name:

____

____

Card type (AmEx, Visa, etc.): ____________________

Account number: ____________________________

Account online username: ______________________

Password: ________________________________

Credit card company name:

____

____

Card type (AmEx, Visa, etc.): ____________________

Account number: ____________________________

Account online username: ______________________

Password: ________________________________

Credit card company name:

____

____

Card type (AmEx, Visa, etc.): ________________________

Account number: ______________________________

Account online username: ________________________

Password: __________________________________

Credit card company name:

____

____

Card type (AmEx, Visa, etc.): ________________________

Account number: ______________________________

Account online username: ________________________

Password: __________________________________

My investment accounts:

Company/Firm name...

Investment/Account type:

Contact name:

Contact number:

Account number:

Account online username:

Password:

Notes:

Company/Firm name...

Investment/Account type:

Contact name:

Contact number:

Account number:

Account online username:

Password:

Notes:

Company/Firm name...

Investment/Account type:

Contact name:

Contact number:

Account number:

Account online username:

Password:

Notes:

Company/Firm name...

Investment/Account type:

Contact name:

Contact number:

Account number:

Account online username:

Password:

Notes:

Safe deposit box:

Bank name:

____

Location:

____

____

____

Safe deposit box number: ______________________

The location of the key: ______________________

Contents: ______________________________________

____

____

____

____

____

Debts or judgements owed to me:

Company or individual...

Contact number:

Location of documents and other notes:

Company or individual...

Contact number:

Location of documents and other notes:

Company or individual...

Contact number:

Location of documents and other notes:

Company or individual...

Contact number:

Location of documents and other notes:

Company or individual...

Contact number:

Location of documents and other notes:

Company or individual...

Contact number:

Location of documents and other notes:

"Somebody should
tell us, right
at the start of our lives,
that we are dying.
Then we might
live life to the limit,
every minute
of every day."
– Pope Paul VI

My Dependents:

This area is for documenting the names and information of people you take care of. This could be children, aging parents, or someone else whose care you are responsible for.

Name: ______________________________

Relationship: ______________________________

Telephone Number: ______________________________

Address: ______________________________

____

Birthplace and birthdate: ______________________________

Guardian name and information: ______________________________

____

Important information regarding this individual:

____

____

____

____

Name: ______________________________

Relationship: ______________________________

Telephone Number: ______________________________

Address: ______________________________

____

Birthplace and birthdate: ______________________________

Guardian name and information: ______________________________

____

Important information regarding this individual:

____

____

____

____

Name: ______________________________

Relationship: ______________________________

Telephone Number: ______________________________

Address: ______________________________

____

Birthplace and birthdate: ______________________________

Guardian name and information: ______________________________

____

Important information regarding this individual:

____

____

____

____

Name: ______________________________

Relationship: ______________________________

Telephone Number: ______________________________

Address: ______________________________

____

Birthplace and birthdate: ______________________________

Guardian name and information: ______________________________

____

Important information regarding this individual:

____

____

____

____

Name: ______________________________

Relationship: ______________________________

Telephone Number: ______________________________

Address: ______________________________

____

Birthplace and birthdate: ______________________________

Guardian name and information: ______________________________

____

Important information regarding this individual:

____

____

____

____

My Pets:

This area is for documenting the names and information of your pets and who will take care of them in case you are unable.

Pet Name: ______________________________

Type of Animal: ______________________________

The person who will take care of them in case you are unable:

Name: ______________________________

Address: ______________________________

____

____

Important information regarding this pet:

____

____

____

Pet Name: ______________________________

Type of Animal: ______________________________

The person who will take care of them in case you are unable:

Name: ______________________________

Address: ______________________________

____

____

Important information regarding this pet:

____

____

____

"Every man's life ends the same way. It is only the details of how he lived and how he died that distinguish one man from another."

– Ernest Hemingway

My Instructions for When I Pass

This section provides you a place to share with your loved ones information regarding the disposition of your remains and how you would like your life to be celebrated.

While this process can be a daunting mental and emotional exercise, it can provide direction and relief to your loved ones. If completed with thoughtfulness and specifics, this section can help give your family comfort by understanding and knowing your wishes.

This is a gift to them, making a difficult time a bit easier. Knowing what you want lets them focus on grieving and celebrating your life and their love for you.

This section includes areas to consider giving details on, such as if you prefer burial, cremation, or something else. It also includes space and guidance for you to express your wishes on how you would like to be memorialized. It provides an opportunity to write your own eulogy and obituary. Lastly, it provides the contact information for whom you would like to be notified of your passing.

Planning Your Celebration of You

Thinking about and planning one's own funeral can be odd and uncomfortable.

No matter how you feel about this task, it is important to consider how planning now can help your loved ones later. The more information your family has about your wishes, the fewer decisions they will have to make when you pass. This allows them to focus on their grief.

These occasions of resolution and celebration come in many forms and formats, letting you tailor yours to fit your values and personality.

It can be a formal or casual affair. You can have an enormous event or something more intimate. It can take place in a favorite spot or in a traditional religious setting.

It's the celebration of your life, so you get to decide the details.

Loved ones have grieved the passing of a loved one with everything from marching bands to doves being released to attendees wearing costumes.

They have played video footage and have broadcast ceremonies across the internet. There is one story I read of a scavenger hunt a family held for strategically placed mementos.

The key is to make it fit you and your wants, while also giving your loved ones a way to celebrate you and your life and grieve your passing.

While not exclusive, the ceremonies we typically associate with someone's passing are funerals, graveside services, memorial services, and celebrations-of-life.

Funerals are often traditional and religious and are comprised of one or all the following: a visitation, a funeral service, and a committal service.

The visitation, or viewing, occurs before the funeral and is when attendees pay their respects to the reposed and family.

The traditional setting for a funeral service is a church or funeral home, and is presided over by a pastor, priest, or funeral director. They tend to be formal and comprised of music (usually hymns), prayers, and readings from scripture.

A committal service occurs at the gravesite and is usually religious in tone, with an officiant leading the attendees in comments, readings, prayers, and song. It can also be part of a cremation, with it occurring at the crematorium or at the burial of ashes.

A graveside service differs from a committal service by being less religious. These services often have eulogies from loved ones, the singing or playing of favorite songs, and flowers being placed on the coffin to say goodbye.

A memorial service can be religious or secular and do not have the coffin present. They can occur in both traditional places like a church or funeral home or in untraditional ones such as a home, community center, or outdoors.

Celebration-of-life ceremonies are flexible in structure and provide room to express the deceased's life and personality. There are fewer expectations and traditions, making creativity and budget the only limitations on venue and program.

The key is to focus on what best reflects you, while also providing an opportunity for your family and friends to celebrate you and your life and say their goodbyes.

In case of my death, these are my wishes:

The person or persons I have asked to be responsible for carrying out my wishes is:

Make my arrangements with this funeral home (include address):

I would like my remains to be (buried, cremated, or something else):

____

____

My preference for the type of service I want is (check all that match your wishes):

- ☐ A visitation
- ☐ A funeral service
- ☐ A committal service
- ☐ A graveside service
- ☐ A memorial service
- ☐ A celebration-of-life
- ☐ A reception (also called a repast)
- ☐ Other events:

  ____

  ____

When I think about how my life is celebrated and remembered, the character and tone I want is (serious, somber, religious, formal, informal, lively, etc.) ...

When I think about how my life is celebrated and remembered, my wish for the number of attendees is (intimate, just immediate family, whoever wants to come can come, my family and friends can decide, etc.) ...

I would like this person to serve as officiant of the services:

If this person is not available, my second choice is:

I would like eulogies to be given by:

And these people to deliver prayers, poems, or other readings:

The passages I would like them to read are (specify bible verses, book passages, letters you have written, etc.):

I would like these songs, hymns, or other pieces of music to be played:

I would like these individuals to serve as pallbearers (if used):

In lieu of flowers or gifts, I would like donations to go to:

I would like these individuals notified:

My clergyperson/spiritual contact:

- Name: ______________________________

- Telephone number: ______________________________

The executor of my will:

- Name: ______________________________

- Telephone number: ______________________________

My personal physician:

- Name: ______________________________

- Telephone number: ______________________________

My health care agent:

- Name: ______________________________

- Telephone number: ______________________________

My employer:

- Name: ______________________________

- Telephone number: ______________________________

These groups and organizations:

- Group/Organization name:

  ____

  ____

- Contact name: ______________________________
- Telephone number: ___________________________
- Group/Organization name:

  ____

  ____

- Contact name: ______________________________
- Telephone number: ___________________________
- Group/Organization name:

  ____

  ____

- Contact name: ______________________________
- Telephone number: ___________________________

These family & friends:

Name: ____

Relationship: ____

Telephone Number(s): _______________________________

Email Address: _______________________________________

Address: ____

____

____

Name: ____

Relationship: ____

Telephone Number(s): _______________________________

Email Address: _______________________________________

Address: ____

____

____

Name: ____

Relationship: ______________________________________

Telephone Number(s): ________________________________

Email Address: ______________________________________

Address: ____

____

____

Name: ____

Relationship: ______________________________________

Telephone Number(s): ________________________________

Email Address: ______________________________________

Address: ____

____

____

Name: ______________________________

Relationship: ______________________________

Telephone Number(s): ______________________________

Email Address: ______________________________

Address: ______________________________

____

____

Name: ______________________________

Relationship: ______________________________

Telephone Number(s): ______________________________

Email Address: ______________________________

Address: ______________________________

____

____

Name: ______________________________

Relationship: ______________________________

Telephone Number(s): ______________________________

Email Address: ______________________________

Address: ______________________________

____

____

Name: ______________________________

Relationship: ______________________________

Telephone Number(s): ______________________________

Email Address: ______________________________

Address: ______________________________

____

____

Name: ___________________________________

Relationship: ______________________________

Telephone Number(s): _________________________

Email Address: _____________________________

Address: __________________________________

____

____

Name: ___________________________________

Relationship: ______________________________

Telephone Number(s): _________________________

Email Address: _____________________________

Address: __________________________________

____

____

Name: ____

Relationship: ____

Telephone Number(s): _________________________________

Email Address: _______________________________________

Address: ____

____

____

Name: ____

Relationship: ____

Telephone Number(s): _________________________________

Email Address: _______________________________________

Address: ____

____

____

Name: ____________________

Relationship: ____________________

Telephone Number(s): ____________________

Email Address: ____________________

Address: ____________________

____

____

Name: ____________________

Relationship: ____________________

Telephone Number(s): ____________________

Email Address: ____________________

Address: ____________________

____

____

Name: ____

Relationship: ____________________________________

Telephone Number(s): _____________________________

Email Address: ___________________________________

Address: ____

____

____

Name: ____

Relationship: ____________________________________

Telephone Number(s): _____________________________

Email Address: ___________________________________

Address: ____

____

____

Name: ______________________________

Relationship: ______________________________

Telephone Number(s): ______________________________

Email Address: ______________________________

Address: ______________________________

____

____

Name: ______________________________

Relationship: ______________________________

Telephone Number(s): ______________________________

Email Address: ______________________________

Address: ______________________________

____

____

Name: ______________________________

Relationship: ______________________________

Telephone Number(s): ______________________________

Email Address: ______________________________

Address: ______________________________

____

____

Name: ______________________________

Relationship: ______________________________

Telephone Number(s): ______________________________

Email Address: ______________________________

Address: ______________________________

____

____

Name: ____

Relationship: ____

Telephone Number(s): _________________________________

Email Address: ______________________________________

Address: ____

____

____

Name: ____

Relationship: ____

Telephone Number(s): _________________________________

Email Address: ______________________________________

Address: ____

____

____

Writing Your Own Eulogy

This is the part of the book where you can write your own eulogy.

The thought of doing this may feel odd and possibly morbid. That's understandable, as most of us avoid contemplating our exit from this life.

So why should you write your own eulogy? The same reason you would write your wedding vows: so the words said match how you think and feel.

The typical eulogy involves someone close to the departed giving a speech full of their remembrances, their experiences, and their farewell. Writing your own eulogy allows you to turn this around, making it your memories, your sentiments, and your goodbye.

It's your life, and you are the best person to tell the story. Use this as an opportunity for candor and lead with your heart and avoid humility and exaggeration. Tell your loved ones how much you love them. Thank them for all they gave to your life. While you're at it, give your apologies and forgive your enemies.

Your words will be the gift the people you love will need. They will also be a gift to yourself.

In this writing process, thinking about things done and not done can be the jolt you need to experience more of this life. Your choices become bolder, and you waste less of your time. You replace regrets about yesterday and worries about tomorrow with living the magic of right now.

What to Include in Your Eulogy:

The following are ideas to possibly cover in what you write:

- Where did you grow up?
- What were the highpoints of your growing up years? Talk about school, friends, activities, and favorite memories.
- What are your proudest accomplishments? What did it mean to you to achieve them? Why did they mean so much?
- Who had a major impact on you when you were growing up? What were their specific impacts?
- Think about the significant relationships of your life. Who were they with? How did they change you and what did they add to your life? Write about a few favorite memories.

- What are the biggest lessons you can share about relationships? Why are they important? What can we do to be better spouses, partners, parents, and friends?
- Talk about your career and work. What are the lessons you can share about the role of work in who we are and how we choose to live our lives?
- What were your favorite activities and hobbies?
- What are the reasons behind the choices you made on the way you lived, worked, and expressed yourself?
- What role did faith play in your life and your choices? How does the impermanence of life affect your faith?
- What do you think is the purpose of life? Are our lives the result of fate or free will?
- What lessons can you share on being a better member of a family and a community?
- How do you want to be remembered? Is it for what you achieved or who you helped? Is it for how you were as a parent or a spouse? For how you served your community? Your faith? Your values?

- What were you grateful for? What are the things big and small that made your life incredible?
- What were your favorite things about life? What would you have wanted more time to do and experience?
- What will people miss the most about you? Is it your humor, your art, your cooking, how you loved, or for the friend you were?

My Eulogy:

About Me

"Every death is like the burning of a library."
– Alex Haley

The first two sections of this book have focused on helping you organize your affairs and communicate your wishes in case something happens to you.

This section provides a place for you to write about your life experiences. Through the use of questions and prompts, you will be guided through your memories, making it simple to reminisce and share those stories.

This part of the book is just as important as the rest.

While your family will be relieved that you organized your affairs and eased a time of grief, they will also be eternally grateful to have this collection of your memories.

Sharing your life stories gives your family a thoughtful way to remember you and create a legacy for years to come. It also provides a way for others to better understand how we became who we are. They can better understand the roots of our beliefs and how we see the world.

Think of yourself as a painting. People walk by and all they have is what they can see.

That would change if they had watched the picture being painted. Witnessing the brush strokes and dabs of color transform a blank canvas to a picture on the wall would give them a deeper connection to the painting, a deeper appreciation. They would see it differently, better understanding what is in front of them.

That happens when you share your life stories. These glimpses of what formed you create empathy and connection. It makes the memory of you and your life a book filled with story after story to be shared for generations.

“The mystery of
human existence
lies not in
just staying alive,
but in
finding something
to live for.”
– Fyodor Dostoyevsky

About Me: My Birth and Me as a Baby

My birthdate and birthplace:

I was born at this location (hospital, at home, side of the road):

The reason my birth name was selected:

If I had been asked, I would have chosen this name:

My weight and length at birth were:

My parents' ages when I was born were:

My first words were:

I was this age when I took my first steps:

The details I have been told about the day I was born are:

(If Adopted)

I was adopted when I was this age:

I was this age when I found out I had been adopted:

The way I found out was:

The details I know about my birth parents are:

"The two
most important days
in life
are the day
you are born and
the day
you discover
the reason why."
– Mark Twain

About Me: A Few Things

If I were to write an autobiography, the title would be...

One of my favorite quotes is...

The values I have tried to live my life by are...

I am who I am today in large part because of these experiences...

And these people...

“The meaning
of life is
to find your gift.
The purpose
of life is
to give it away.”
– Picasso

About Me: Memories of My Childhood

When I was a kid, most people called me by this name:

And sometimes this nickname:

I was given that nickname because...

I would describe myself when I was a kid this way...

...and my childhood this way...

When I was a kid, I remember playing these games...

And with these toys...

Watching these movies...

Loving these songs...

And reading these books...

During my elementary school years, my best friends were...

The elementary school teacher I most fondly remember is...

This is what I most remember about them...

When I was a kid, my regular chores included...

In return for doing these tasks, I received an allowance of...

When I was a kid, I dreamed of becoming a...

If I could be a kid again for just one day, I would...

One of my most favorite childhood memories is...

"The purpose of life,
after all, is to live it,
to taste experience
to the utmost,
to reach out
eagerly and without fear
for newer and
richer experience."
– Eleanor Roosevelt

About Me: My High School Years

I would describe myself when I was a teenager this way...

This is how I dressed and styled my hair in my high school years...

When I was a teenager, I loved these bands/musicians...

And these songs...

And these movies and television shows...

And these books...

During my teenage years, my closest friends were...

My parents' opinion of my choice in friends was...

A typical weekend night during my high school years was spent...

I got my driver's license when I was this age...

To get my license, I had to take my driving test this many times...

The principal person who taught me how to drive was...

The car I learned to drive in was a (year, make, and model) ...

I got my first car when I was this age...

My first car was a (year, make, and model) ...

The year I graduated from high school was...

My graduating class had this many students in it...

My grades were typically in this range...

My favorite and least favorite subjects were...

The school activities and sports that I participated in were...

The things I liked about high school were...

...and these are the things I disliked...

Knowing what I know now, the advice I would give my teenage self is...

A teacher, coach, or mentor that had a huge impact on me becoming who I am today is...

The specific influences they had on me and my life were...

"It's not enough
to have lived.
We should
be determined
to live
for something."
– Winston Churchill

About Me: Next Steps

After high school I made the choice to...

☐ Start college.

☐ Join the military.

☐ Get a job.

☐ Take a break.

☐ Other: ________________________________

I made this decision because...

____

____

____

____

When I look back, this is how I now feel about my decision...

☐ It was the right one, at the right time.

☐ It was the right direction to go in, but the wrong time to do it.

☐ You can't get them all right.

☐ The jury's still out.

The reason I think this was the correct or incorrect decision is...

If I had a redo, I would make these changes to this period of my life...

I got my first job when I was this age...

The job was...

So far, the total number of jobs I have had in my lifetime is...

A few of my favorite jobs include...

The first time I truly felt like an adult was...

These are the places where I have lived during my life, including when and why I moved to each one...

"Perhaps they
are not the stars, but
rather openings in
Heaven where the love
of our lost ones pours
through and shines
down upon us
to let us know
they are happy."
– Author Unknown

About Me: My Parents

My mother's full name is...

...and her maiden name is...

This is where she was born...

...and where she grew up...

Her family was from this/these part(s) of the world...

Her highest level of schooling was...

And her occupations were...

The way I would describe my mother is...

She was good at many things, but was especially talented and skilled at...

The ways my mom and I were/are alike are...

And this is how we were/are different...

One of my favorite memories of my mother is...

Some of the best advice she gave me was...

My father's full name is...

His mother's maiden name was...

This is where he was born...

...and where he grew up...

His family was from this/these part(s) of the world...

His highest level of schooling was...

And his occupations were...

The way I would describe my father is...

He was good at many things, but was especially talented and skilled at...

The ways my father and I were/are alike are...

And this is how we were/are different...

One of my favorite memories of my father is...

Some of the best advice he gave me was...

The story of the way my parents met is...

They were married on this date...

Their ages when they were married were...

I would describe their relationship this way...

A list of people other than my parents who helped raise me includes...

"All we have
to decide is
what to do
with the time
that is given us."
– J.R.R. Tolkien,
The Fellowship of the Ring

About Me: My Grandparents

My grandparents' names on my mother's side are...

My maternal grandmother's maiden name was...

I called them...

This is when and where they were born and where they grew up...

Their highest level of schooling was...

Their occupations were...

I would describe my grandparents on my mother's side this way...

My grandparents' names on my father's side are...

My paternal grandmother's maiden name was...

I called them...

This is when and where they were born and where they grew up...

Their highest level of schooling was...

Their occupations were...

I would describe my grandparents on my father's side this way...

A favorite memory of my grandparents is...

"You are braver than you believe, stronger than you seem, and smarter than you think."

– A.A. Milne, Winnie the Pooh

About Me: My Siblings

I have this many brothers and sisters...

I am the oldest/middle/youngest or only child...

My siblings' names and birthdates are...

A letter to my siblings...

A letter to my siblings...

A letter to my siblings...

A letter to my siblings...

"Love
doesn't make
the world go 'round.
Love
is what
makes the ride
worthwhile."
– Franklin P. Jones

About Me: My Marriage/My Partner

I have been married or had a long-term partner this many times...

The story of how I met my current partner/spouse is...

The story of how I proposed/was proposed to is...

This is the date we were married...

This is what our wedding was like...

My favorite memory of a time with my spouse/partner is...

“Parent:
an example of a word
that is a noun
before you
are one
and a verb
after you are.”
– Author Unknown

About Me: My Children

I was this age when I first decided that one day, I wanted to have kids...

And I was this age when I first became a parent...

My child's/children's names and dates of birth/adoption are...

Their first words were...

And they were these ages when they took their first steps...

When they were little, I remember reading these books to them...

And singing these songs to them...

Looking back, the biggest changes I would make in how I raised my kids is...

The best parts of being a parent are...

And the hardest parts of being a parent are...

"Your children
are your
rainbows and
your grandchildren
are your
pot of gold."
– Author Unknown

About Me: My Grandchildren

I was this age when I became a grandparent...

____

I have this many grandkids...

____

My grandkids' names and ages are...

This is what I remember about the first time I was told I was going to be a grandparent...

The most surprising thing about being a grandparent is...

In my opinion the biggest difference between being a parent and a grandparent is...

The best part of being a grandparent is...

"Three things in human
life are important:
The first is
to be kind.
The second is
to be kind.
And the third is
to be kind."
– Henry James

About Me: My Life Experiences

- ☐ Traveled overseas.
- ☐ Flown in a plane.
- ☐ Milked a cow.
- ☐ Been in a fist fight.
- ☐ Gone on a blind date.
- ☐ Made a speech in front of a large group.
- ☐ Sung a solo in front of an audience.
- ☐ Ridden a motorcycle.
- ☐ Shot a gun.
- ☐ Taken a ride in a hot air balloon.
- ☐ Gone on a cruise.
- ☐ Gone scuba diving.
- ☐ Run a marathon.
- ☐ Gone bungee jumping.
- ☐ Skipped school.
- ☐ Ridden in a helicopter.
- ☐ Gotten a tattoo.
- ☐ Attended a Broadway musical.
- ☐ Used a fake ID.

- ☐ Been to a professional sporting event.
- ☐ Met a celebrity.
- ☐ Gone skydiving.
- ☐ Been to a large music festival.
- ☐ Gone surfing.
- ☐ Performed in a play, musical, or opera.
- ☐ Gone backpacking.
- ☐ Snuck into a movie.
- ☐ Gotten a speeding ticket.
- ☐ Gotten out of a speeding ticket.
- ☐ Been selected for a jury.
- ☐ Been in a band.
- ☐ Performed CPR or the Heimlich Maneuver on someone.
- ☐ Driven in a country where they drive on the other side of the road.
- ☐ Seen a meteor shower.
- ☐ Been stuck in an elevator.
- ☐ Gone ice skating.
- ☐ Gone snow skiing.
- ☐ Been to a tropical island.

- ☐ Ridden in a train.
- ☐ Experienced an earthquake.
- ☐ Been in a hurricane.
- ☐ Been where a tornado struck down.
- ☐ Lived in a foreign country.
- ☐ Gone sailing.
- ☐ Been to a rodeo.
- ☐ Gone deep sea fishing.
- ☐ Driven a tractor.
- ☐ Ridden in a horse-drawn carriage.
- ☐ Ridden a mechanical bull.
- ☐ Been a passenger in a private jet.
- ☐ Had my picture taken with someone famous.
- ☐ Been a maid of honor/best man.
- ☐ Been on television.
- ☐ Seen a UFO.
- ☐ Participated in a political protest.
- ☐ Attended the ballet.
- ☐ Attended the opera.

My first trip out of the country was to...

The first ocean I ever saw was...

The first time I ever saw snow was...

If I could live anywhere in the world for a year with all expenses paid, I would choose to live here...

My favorite travel memory is...

A few of my favorite places I have traveled to are...

The religious and spiritual practices that are a part of my daily life are...

The ways my spiritual and religious practices have changed and evolved over the course of my life are...

If I had to choose between fate or free will, I believe this one has the biggest impact on our lives:

A miracle I have personally experienced is...

When times are tough, this is how I give myself the inner-strength I need...

"He is
a wise man
who does not grieve
for the things
which he has not,
but rejoices
for those
which he has."
– Epictetus

I Am Grateful For...

This risk I took:

This sacrifice I made:

This big change I made in my life:

This piece of advice I was given:

This lesson I learned the "hard way:"

This thing that I really wanted to happen but didn't:

While challenges and failure can sap our hopes and weaken our outlook, they can also provide the motivation needed to make key life changes and decisions. Looking back, a few of the things that caused hardship but later led to positive transformations, are...

"It is not death
that a man
should fear,
but he should fear
never beginning
to live."
– Marcus Aurelius

Letters

Write personal notes to specific loved ones in your life.

A letter to: ______________________________

A letter to: ____________________

A letter to: ______________________________

A letter to: ______

A letter to: ______

A letter to: ____________________

A letter to: ______________________________

A letter to: ______________________________

A letter to: ____

A letter to: ______________________________

A letter to: ______________________________

Glossary

Advance Care Directive:

A legal document that communicates your preferences regarding your medical care. Your medical providers would use the document if you become incapacitated and cannot advocate for yourself.

Beneficiary:

The person, persons, or organizations that are the recipients of a legal Will or Trust.

Burial:

The act where the deceased is placed into the ground.

Celebration of Life:

Like a funeral or memorial service, with the primary exception that a celebration of life event often happens after final disposition has occurred. Because these events typically occur after burial or cremation, they provide for more flexibility, planning, and creativity.

Cardiopulmonary Resuscitation (CPR):

A lifesaving measure used for when someone's breathing and/or heartbeat have stopped working.

Conservatorship:

A legal arrangement that gives an adult the court-ordered authority and responsibility to manage another adult's financial affairs.

Cremation:

An act and practice of final disposition, where the remains are reduced to their essential elements with the use of combustion and high temperatures.

Digital Accounts:

These are online accounts used for activities such as social media, online shopping, and getting information. Does not include the items or data stored within an account, such as photos or financial assets that are accessed online.

Digital Account Manager (s):

The person(s) you appoint to manage or shut down your social media and other online accounts. Not a legal role.

They are not the owner of the accounts or their contents. Items stored online (photos, investments, finances, etc.) should have specific instructions on their distribution in your will.

Do Not Intubate Order (DNI):

Legal document declining cardiopulmonary resuscitation (CPR) or other measures to prolong or save your life.

Do Not Resuscitate Order (DNR):

Document that states your wishes for what your medical care team should or should not do to prolong or save your life.

Durable Power of Attorney for Health Care:

A legal document giving another individual legal permission to make medical decisions on your behalf in the event you cannot make them yourself. The laws where you live dictate the official title of the person, with the most common being agent, attorney-in-fact, health care proxy, or patient advocate.

Estate:

The total accumulation of an individual's assets. A probate estate is the sum of all assets processed in a probate or court hearing. A trust estate is all assets held by a trust. A taxable estate is all assets that are subject to estate tax.

Estate Plan:

An estate plan manages the disposition of a person's property according to their wishes before or after their death.

Executor:
The person that administers a deceased person's estate by following the Last Will and Testament.

Fiduciary:
A person or entity with the legal duty to act primarily for another's benefit.

Funeral:
A ceremony to honor someone who has passed. Often spiritual or religious. Typically, more formal and structured than a memorial service or celebration of life.

Guardian:
Someone given the legal authority to make healthcare decisions and to manage property and financial matters on behalf of another person. The court can appoint a guardian in the absence of a healthcare agent.

Holographic Will
A handwritten will.

Joint Will (also called a Conjoint Will)
A will that covers two or more individual's assets.

Last Will of Testament

A legal document dictating what happens to your assets and/or the custody of dependents upon your death.

Letter of Wishes:

Used as part of a trust to pass along additional instructions to the trustees. A letter of wishes is easier to change than a will or trust deed. While not legally binding, it must be considered and is usually followed during probate.

Living Trust:

A living trust dictates the distribution of assets after you die. Examples of assets that can be placed in a trust are property, bank accounts, and investments. The living trust is the legal owner of the property placed in it with you keeping control. Unlike a will, items in a trust don't go through probate.

Memorial Service:

A celebration of someone's life and an acknowledgement of their passing. A big distinction from a funeral service is that the deceased is not present.

Mystic Will

A will kept sealed until the individual has passed.

Officiant:

The person who leads a service or ceremony, such as a marriage or burial. Depending on where the event occurs, an officiant may be religious or secular in title and position.

Organ Donor:

A person or entity with the legal duty to act primarily for another's benefit.

Pallbearer:

Person assigned to carry the casket during a funeral service.

Physician Orders for Life Sustaining Treatment (POLST):

A legal form signed by you and your doctor that details your wishes for medical treatment and life-resuscitation measures attempted.

Power of Attorney:

A document that gives another person legal authority to act on your behalf. If you create such a document, you are called the principal, and the person to whom you give this authority is called your agent or attorney-in-fact. If you make a durable power of attorney, the document will continue in effect even if you become incapacitated.

Preplanning:
The practice of working with an advisor or funeral home to record your wishes for final disposition. While not required, it can also involve prepaying for the event and disposition.

Probate:
The court process following a person's death that includes:

- authenticating the deceased person's will.
- naming a designee to handle the deceased person's affairs.
- identifying and inventorying the deceased person's estate.
- providing for the payment of all debts and taxes.
- distributing assets as directed by a will or state law if there is no will.

Probate Estate:
The portion of your total assets distributed via probate.

Reception (also known as a repast):
An informal gathering after a funeral service. Often held at a funeral home, residence, restaurant, or other venue.

Settlor:
The entity or person who creates a legal trust.

Serviceman's Will:

The will of a person in active-duty military service.

Taxable Estate:

All assets that are subject to an estate tax.

Trust:

A legal agreement where property is held and managed by a Trustee.

Trust Estate:

A substate of your estate or all total assets. A trust estate includes all assets held by a trust.

Trustee:

The person or company that manages a trust on behalf of the beneficiary.

Unsolemn Will:

A will where the executor is unknown. In these cases, the court appoints an executor.

Will:

A legal document stating the intentions of a deceased person concerning the distribution of their property.

Hear Your Story Books

At **Hear Your Story**, we have crafted a line of guided journals to give each of us a place to tell the unique stories of who we are, where we have been, and where we are going.

Hearing and reading the stories of the people in our lives creates closeness, appreciation, and understanding. It strengthens our bonds and gives the people in our lives a way to share with us their legacy and their memories.

Available at Amazon,

all bookstores, and HearYourStory.com

Hear Your Story Books

- Mom, I Want to Hear Your Story: A Mother's Guided Journal to Share Her Life & Her Love
- Dad, I Want to Hear Your Story: A Father's Guided Journal to Share His Life & His Love
- Grandmother, I Want to Hear Your Story: A Grandmother's Guided Journal to Share Her Life and Her Love
- Grandfather, I Want to Hear Your Story: A Grandfather's Guided Journal to Share His Life and His Love

- Tell Your Life Story: The Write Your Own Autobiography Guided Journal
- The Story of Expecting You: A Selfcare Pregnancy Guided Journal and Memory Book
- Life Gave Me You; I Want to Hear Your Story: A Guided Journal for Stepmothers to Share Their Life Story
- You Choose to Be My Dad; I Want to Hear Your Story: A Guided Journal for Stepdads to Share Their Life Story
- To My Wonderful Aunt, I Want to Hear Your Story: A Guided Journal to Share Her Life and Her Love
- To My Uncle, I Want to Hear Your Story: A Guided Journal to Share His Life and His Love
- Love Notes: I Wrote This Book About You
- Getting to Know You: 201 Fun Questions to Deepen Your Relationship and Hear Each Other's Story
- You, Me, and Us: 229 Fun Relationship Questions to Ask Your Guy or Girl
- Because I Love You: The Couple's Bucket List That Builds Your Relationship

About the Author

Jeffrey Mason brings a life of many experiences to his books. After serving as a Hospital Corpsman with the United States Navy and Marine Corps, he worked in the healthcare, telecommunications, high tech, and government sectors.

To date, Jeffrey has written 23 books, mostly centered around the discovery and sharing of personal and family histories.

This focus inspired him to create **Hear Your Story**, a company with the mission to give everyone a way to reminisce and share the stories of their life, while also creating cherished memories that can be shared for generations.

Hear Your Story donates a percentage of its profits. To date, these contributions have benefitted Alzheimer's research and care, reducing hunger and poverty, and helping kids and teenagers manage depression and social anxiety.

You can contact Jeffrey directly at hello@jeffreymason.com, at hearyourstory.com, or www.jeffreymason.com.
He would be grateful if you would help people to find his books by leaving a review on Amazon. Your feedback helps him get better at this thing he loves.

Made in United States
North Haven, CT
05 November 2026

21772137R00124